# BRITISH CAMPAIGN MEDALS OF THE FIRST WORLD WAR

## Peter Duckers

SHIRE PUBLICATIONS

Published in Great Britain in 2014 by Shire Publications Ltd,
PO Box 883, Oxford OX1 9PL, United Kingdom.
PO Box 3985, New York, NY 10185-3983, USA.
E-mail: shire@shirebooks.co.uk    www.shirebooks.co.uk

A CIP catalogue record for this book is available from the
British Library.

Shire Library no. 636    .    ISBN-13: 978 0 74780 843 5

Peter Duckers has asserted his right under the Copyright,
Designs and Patents Act, 1988, to be identified as the
author of this book.

Designed by Myriam Bell Design, France
Typeset in Perpetua and Gill Sans.
Printed in China through World Print Ltd.

14 15 16 17 18   10 9 8 7 6 5 4 3 2

COVER IMAGE
Design by Peter Ashley. Front cover: British War Medal
1914–20 (Date:1919) with grateful thanks to Philip
French at the Newarke Houses Museum (incorporating the
Museum of the Royal Leicestershire Regiment) Leicester;
photograph by Peter Ashley. Back cover detail: Section of
ribbon from the Victory Medal; photograph Peter Duckers.

TITLE PAGE IMAGE
Part of a group of dress miniatures, showing examples of
the naval clasps, never officially issued.

CONTENTS PAGE IMAGE
A group containing the '1915 trio' with the Mercantile
Marine Medal – the maximum that could be earned for
1914–18 campaign service.

ACKNOWLEDGEMENTS
The majority of the illustrations and awards shown in the
book are from the author's own collection or from the
Shropshire Regimental Museum in Shrewsbury Castle,
used by kind permission of the Trustees. Documents from
The National Archives in Kew (pp. 37, 38, 39, 40) are
reproduced with permission.

EDITOR'S NOTE
Please note that medals are not shown to scale.

Shire Publications is supporting the Woodland Trust, the UK's leading woodland conservation charity, by funding the dedication of trees.

# CONTENTS

# INTRODUCTION

**M**EDALS FOR WAR SERVICE have been awarded in Britain since the sixteenth century, starting with awards for the Armada campaign in 1588. Over the course of the next two hundred years they were issued sporadically, often unofficially or semi-officially, in small numbers to selected individuals, reflecting no standardised system. Modern medallic awards for operational service are given to all those, regardless of rank or distinction, who were present in a particular campaign for a designated length of time. The first mass awards in these broad terms were made by the Honourable East India Company (HEIC), which began to issue campaign medals on a large scale in the 1780s, presenting silver or gold medals to its Indian (but not European) soldiers for the Deccan campaigns of 1778–84. The Company continued to make general awards to its Indian soldiers for all its major campaigns until its abolition in 1858 as a result of the Indian Mutiny.

In purely British terms, the silver medal for the Waterloo campaign of 1815 is usually regarded as the first 'modern' medallic award, since it was given to all those present on the campaign, was hung from a distinctive ribbon, was named to its recipient, and was also presented to the next of kin of those who had died. However, it was not until the period 1839–42, with the large-scale issuing of medals for operations in Afghanistan and for the 'Opium War' with China, that a regulated system of awards came into being. Thereafter, service medals were given to all British forces (and HEIC personnel until 1858) for major operations on land and sea. The idea of clasps – silver bars carried on the medal to indicate the recipient's presence in a major action – originated with the Sutlej Medal for the First Sikh War of 1845–6. As the British Empire expanded between 1850 and 1914 it became standard practice to award campaign medals with clasps as appropriate, so that there are dozens of different types of medal and hundreds of different clasps reflecting British military operations around the world.

From the mid-nineteenth century, campaign medal designs became standardised: most (but not quite all) were circular and of silver, commonly bearing the recipient's details engraved or machine-impressed around the rim.

They usually bore the reigning monarch's effigy and titles on one side (the *obverse*), and a decorative or symbolic design, or sometimes simple wording, on the back (the *reverse*). They were suspended from a coloured ribbon, whose design was distinctive to that medal or campaign.

The First World War was the largest conflict that Britain and her Imperial forces had ever faced, involving operations around the world, on land, at sea and in the air, and drawing in civilian populations on a scale never before seen. The British authorities naturally considered the matter of campaign medals while the war was still being fought. It was clear that those who participated should be rewarded with service medals, as well as with any awards for gallant or distinguished service that individuals might earn.

In terms of a general award, it was first proposed to issue medals with campaign or battle clasps, following the precedent of earlier types. The last major campaign before 1914 had been the South African or 'Boer' War of 1899–1902. This had produced two similar silver medals, one bearing the effigy of Queen Victoria and, since the Queen died while the war was still in progress, another bearing the effigy of her successor, Edward VII. More to the point, the campaign resulted in the authorisation of no fewer than twenty-six separate clasps, reflecting service in large set-piece battles, such as *Paardeberg*, in sieges and reliefs, as at Ladysmith, Kimberley and Mafeking, in larger-scale operations such as those on the *Tugela Heights*, or 'general' service over wider areas such as the Orange Free State or the Transvaal.

In 1919 two committees, Army and Navy, investigated the possibility of producing a campaign medal bearing clasps for service in the First World War. Given the scale of the operations, it is not surprising that the War Office committee proposed no fewer than seventy-nine, and the Admiralty sixty-eight. Proposed Army clasps included those for major operations such as *Somme 1916* and *Gallipoli 1915* and area honours such as *France 1914–15*. The Admiralty's proposals were much the same, with clasps for ship-to-ship actions (recalling the days of Nelson's victories!), such as *Emden 9 November 1914*,

Above left: An early Honourable East India Company medal – the gold award for the Mysore Campaign, 1792.

Above middle: The 'first British war medal', for Waterloo, 1815. It bears the effigy of the Prince Regent (later George IV) reigning in place of his incapacitated father, George III.

Above right: Medals for the First Sikh War (1845–6) (left) and the Second Sikh War (1848–9) (right): the beginnings of standardised medals carrying clasps.

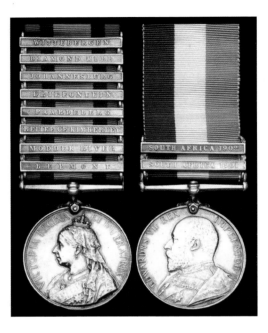

or for major fleet actions such as *Jutland 31 May 1916*, or for operations in support of land service, such as *Belgian Coast* and *Gallipoli Landing*. The wider-ranging naval presence above and below the seas was reflected in 'area' clasps such as *North Sea 1915* and *Home Seas 1918* and in service-specific clasps such as *Marmora Submarines* or *Q Ships*. The addition of these clasps to the medals would have added immensely to their historical and personal interest, but it never happened. The complexity of working out who would be entitled to which clasps – bearing in mind that they would also be given to Imperial forces – and the expense of the project forced its abandonment in 1923. In July 1920, however, the Admiralty published its proposed clasps, so one sometimes sees today, as the only survival of this interesting plan, dress miniatures of the British War Medal bearing naval clasps. These were produced by military tailors anxious to cater for the future demands of their customers and purchased mainly by naval officers for mess dress or formal wear.

Just as the issue of clasps proved too expensive to proceed with, so the range of medals to be awarded was restricted. Instead of separate medals for naval, military and aerial forces or distinctive awards for different theatres of war (such as a proposed 'Gallipoli Star'), it was decided that all eligible recipients would receive essentially the same medals,

Above left: South African War medals, 1899–1902, with examples of the many clasps associated with the awards.

Left: Part of a group of dress miniatures, showing examples of the naval clasps, never officially issued.

regardless of branch of service or theatre of war. A soldier who had served in the Royal Flying Corps in France might receive exactly the same awards as an Indian infantryman for East Africa or an Australian Light Horseman for Palestine or a submariner serving in the Mediterranean. As an extreme example, it was possible for a soldier who had seen only a few weeks' service on the North West Frontier of India in 1915 to wear exactly the same three medals as one who had served for four years on the Western Front. This restriction on the range of awards caused some adverse comment, but it was a logical response to a complicated issue.

Another matter that exercised the attention of the authorities was that of a 'home service' medal. No-one doubted the fairness of awarding medals to those who had fought overseas, but many people served only in the United Kingdom, and the war also drew in the civilian population to an extent never before experienced. Not only were the civilians of Great Britain subjected for the first time to actual attack

'They also served': female ordnance factory workers, 1918. No medal was awarded for civilian war work.

– from warship bombardments to Zeppelin and bomber raids – but they were also involved in the prosecution of the war in many spheres. Since men and women in large numbers were involved in ordnance and weapon production, war transport, nursing and a host of other vital areas of war work, or on home defence duties, a special medal was strongly urged. It was claimed by some that the new Order of the British Empire (1917) – an award made available in a wider range of classes and to many more recipients than the older Orders – went some way to answering this need, but not everyone who had done sterling war work received any such reward. In the end, the sheer scale of the problem proved its downfall; it was simply deemed to be too complicated to work out exactly who should get a home-service medal and on what terms, and too expensive to administer in a time of economic depression. It is interesting that this was not the case in 1945: at the end of the Second World War, the Defence Medal was produced to reward at least some of those who had served within the United Kingdom.

# BRITISH CAMPAIGN MEDALS AWARDED FOR 1914–18

AFTER MUCH DELIBERATION and committee work during and after the war, in the end only six medals were authorised for campaign service in the 'Great War'. One recipient could earn anything from one to four medals but most received two or three, depending on if and when they 'entered a theatre of war'.

### THE 1914 STAR

The first campaign medal authorised for war service was a bronze star. Its issue was the result of pressure by King George V, who ardently believed that the men of 1914 should receive a distinctive award. He repeatedly pressed the matter – despite Army opposition – into the summer of 1917. The Army believed that a simple clasp *1914* on any eventual war medal would be enough, but in the end they acceded to the King's request. The 1914 Star was ultimately authorised for the Army by Special Army Order 350 of 1917, and for the Royal Navy by an Admiralty Fleet Order in January 1918.

Once commonly, and wrongly, called the 'Mons Star', some 378,000 were awarded 'to those serving on the strength of a unit' between 4 August and 22 November 1914. Most went to the professional soldiers of the Regular Army in the original British Expeditionary Force under Sir John French – nicknamed the 'Old Contemptibles' after the sarcastic comment of the Kaiser that the British had 'a contemptible little army' – and to the reinforcements deployed up to midnight on 22–23 November 1914. By then the Allied line had stabilised, and thereafter the war on the Western Front lost its initial mobility and settled down to the attrition of trench warfare. Some Territorial infantry and Yeomanry units did reach the Western Front in time to qualify, and a range of volunteers (nurses, Red Cross, chauffeurs, etc.) also earned the medal.

The uniface bronze award, 62mm high by 44.5mm wide and machine-pressed in one piece, was designed by W. H. J. Blakemore and takes the form of a four-pointed star whose topmost point is obscured by a crown with integral ribbon suspension ring. It is overlaid by a wreath of oakleaves and crossed Roman swords and carries the dates 'Aug – 1914 – Nov' in a scroll across the centre. Perhaps strangely for the first-designed medal for the First World War, it does not bear the royal effigy and titles, though on the lower point a large 'G' encircles a small 'V', representing the monogram of King George V.

The watered ribbon is 32mm wide, in three equal stripes of red, white and blue that merge into each other, and, since it was authorised while the war was in progress, one sometimes sees photographs of soldiers of 1914–18 wearing the ribbon. Presumably, the ribbon is meant to reflect the national colours of Great Britain.

The star is named on its otherwise flat and plain reverse in machine-impressed (not engraved) square block capitals, with considerable variations in size, and usually has the recipient's number, abbreviated rank, initials, surname and abbreviated unit. Those to officers do not carry a service number.

Awards to naval forces are very rare since the medal was not given for service purely at sea; a few were awarded to RN personnel serving ashore (e.g. manning naval armoured trains), but other naval forces received the 1914–15 Star (see below) even if they had been on active service from the earliest days of the war. This lack of a 1914 reward for the Navy – since thousands of sailors had served since August 1914 – caused some criticism. Considerable numbers were, however, awarded to Royal Marine forces and the Royal Naval Divisions, largely those serving in the garrisons defending Dunkirk and Antwerp, where many became prisoners of war or were interned. The Star was also given to the early contingents of Imperial troops arriving on the Western Front, principally in the Indian Army and some Canadians.

The 1914 Star, obverse.

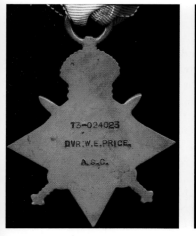

Left: The 1914 Star, reverse, showing typical Army naming style.

Right: Reverse showing naming to an Indian soldier.

9

Those to aerial forces are impressed with 'RFC' or 'RNAS' for the Royal Flying Corps and Royal Naval Air Service respectively; since the RAF was not created until 1918, the medal will not carry that abbreviation. Both are scarce, since the numbers involved were not large. Similarly scarce are awards to female nurses.

The 1914 Star was never awarded by itself; those who received it were automatically entitled to the British War Medal and Victory Medal (*q.v.*), so received three medals, even if their service had been curtailed in 1914 by death, injury or illness.

## THE 1914–15 STAR

Authorised by Special Army Order 20 of 1919 with subsequent amendments, the award is identical to the 1914 Star except that it carries the central dates '1914–15' on a short scroll, in place of 'Aug – 1914 – Nov' as on the earlier award. Its ribbon is also identical to that for the 1914 version – 32mm wide, in equal stripes of red, white and blue that merge into each other.

The award arose out of the much-publicised disquiet felt by those who did not receive the 1914 Star but had been on active service in 1914 (such as the Royal Navy), or had fought in severe campaigns in 1915 which were thought equally worthy of reward. There was a long newspaper campaign over 'distinctive awards' in the manner of the 1914 Star throughout the war. Those who had fought in 1915 demanded their own medal – if there was a 1914 Star for the British Expeditionary Force in France and Flanders, why not something special for the Australians at Gallipoli or the Indians in Mesopotamia or those who had served at Ypres? In fact, a 'Gallipoli Star' was proposed and designed, but in the end the idea of awarding distinctive 'theatre' medals was abandoned.

The 1914–15 Star, obverse, with ribbon.

Instead, it was agreed that this bronze star would be given to those who had not received the 1914 version but had served in 1914 and/or 1915, in whatever service or theatre. It was awarded to all those who served in operations on the Western Front after 22 November 1914 and before 31 December 1915. It was also awarded to those who had served in any other theatre or at sea since 5 August 1914 and before 31 December 1915 – for example, in the campaigns in East Africa, Egypt and Mesopotamia in 1914–15, in Gallipoli and Salonika in 1915, and in smaller theatres such as German West Africa, Persia, the North West Frontier of India, the Pacific and elsewhere. It should be noted, therefore, that recipients of this star could have been in action since the beginning of the war, but only those who served in France and Flanders received the 1914 Star.

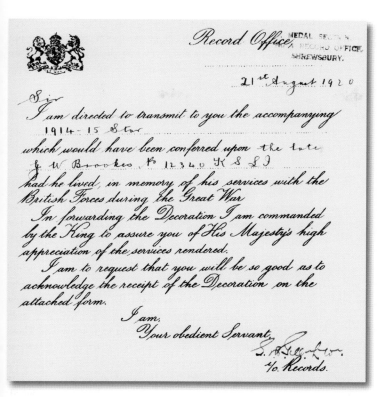

*Record Office,*
MEDAL SECTION
RECORD OFFICE
SHREWSBURY.

*21st August 1920*

Sir,

I am directed to transmit to you the accompanying 1914-15 Star which would have been conferred upon the late J. W. Brookes No 12340 K S L I had he lived, in memory of his services with the British Forces during the Great War

In forwarding the Decoration I am commanded by the King to assure you of His Majesty's high appreciation of the services rendered.

I am to request that you will be so good as to acknowledge the receipt of the Decoration on the attached form.

I am,
Your obedient Servant,
S. A. Leighton.
⅌/o. Records.

The 1914–15 Star: an official transmission slip, sending the award. Each had an attached receipt, to be returned by the recipient. This one is named to a deceased soldier and would have been forwarded to the known next of kin.

The medal was awarded to land, sea and aerial forces, to Imperial forces and to designated civilian categories (e.g. some nursing services). Around 2,366,000 were issued, with approximately 284,000 to naval forces, making it one of the most frequently seen British medals. The Star could not be awarded by itself; as with the 1914 Star, any recipient was automatically entitled to the British War Medal and Victory Medal, so would receive three medals, even if he or she had been killed or died in 1914–15, or their service had been curtailed by wounds, illness or injuries before the end of the war.

The Star is named on the otherwise flat and plain reverse. As with the 1914 Star, naming details are machine-impressed (not engraved), usually giving the recipient's number, abbreviated rank, initials, surname and abbreviated unit. Those to officers do not carry a service number. Awards to naval forces and marines do not carry a ship's name, but simply the branch abbreviation such as 'RN', 'RNVR', 'MFA', 'RNR', 'RMLI' etc. (with a naval recipient's rank coming after the surname), whilst those to aerial forces are impressed with 'RFC' or 'RNAS'; the RAF was not created until 1918, so the Star will not carry that abbreviation.

The 1914–15 Star: detail of the obverse, showing typical Royal Navy naming style, with rank given after the surname.

Below: The 1914 Star with dated clasp, stitched to the ribbon.

Bottom: The dated clasp to the 1914 Star. The reverse is flat and unmarked.

Obviously, those who had earned the 1914 Star would not be eligible for the 1914–15 Star, so no-one could wear both, but it nevertheless caused considerable criticism that the later Star was to all intents identical to the earlier one; this was one reason why a clasp (see below) was belatedly added to the 1914 Star, to provide some visible difference between the two awards, and to honour those who had been under fire early in the war.

## THE DATED CLASP TO THE 1914 STAR

There was criticism of the fact that the 1914 Star and the 1914–15 Star were almost identical. The 'Old Contemptibles', and others who had been at the front since the early days of the war, felt, perhaps understandably, that their award was diminished because of its similarity to a medal that could have been earned for service over a year later than theirs, or because the 1914 Star could also be awarded for service far behind the fighting lines (e.g. in hospitals and depots near the coast).

This was one reason for the authorisation of the only clasp to a 1914–18 campaign medal: a dated bar to be worn on the ribbon of the 1914 Star – despite the fact that the original Army Order for the 1914 Star had specifically stated that 'no clasp will be issued' with the medal. Authorised by Army Order 361 of 19 October 1919, amended in 1920 and 1921, the clasp rewarded all those who had been 'under the close fire of the enemy' prior to midnight of 22–23 November 1914, this being defined as 'within range of the enemy's mobile artillery'.

Made in bronze and measuring only 31mm by 5mm, the clasp bears the dates '5ᵀᴴ Aᴜɢ – 22ᴺᴰ Nᴏᴠ 1914' and was simply stitched on to the ribbon of the medal. This insecure attachment must have resulted in the loss of many clasps but was forced by the shape of the Star, which did not allow the usual attachment to the suspension. Some are seen with a back-strap allowing the clasp to be slid over the ribbon – a better idea – but these are unofficial types, possibly made by military tailors, though at least some were available via the British Legion.

Those who were still serving when the clasp was authorised in 1919 had to claim via their commanding officer, whilst those who had left the services, or relatives claiming on behalf of deceased personnel, claimed on an official form made widely available (e.g. at post offices). A problem lay in the fact that the claim to service *under fire* prior to 22 November 1914 often had to be verified. Since many potential officer and NCO witnesses were dead by 1919, or dispersed and difficult to trace, there must have been many who were never able to support their claim and many who simply

The 1914 'trio' with dated bar on the 1914 Star.

Ribbon bar or 'strip' showing the 1914 Star ribbon carrying the silver rosette, indicating the award of the dated 1914 clasp.

never bothered. The clasp is therefore somewhat scarcer than it probably ought to be, with about 345,000 awarded.

When ribbons are worn alone, the possession of the 1914 clasp is denoted by a small silver rosette worn in the centre of the 1914 Star ribbon. It is, however, quite common to see the rosette incorrectly worn on the full-size ribbon, sometimes along with the actual clasp or sometimes replacing one that has been lost. On the Medal Index Cards (see page 36), the award of the clasp and accompanying rosette is indicated by the words 'clasp and roses'.

## THE BRITISH WAR MEDAL (BWM)

This circular medal, 36mm in diameter, was essentially the basic service award for the First World War, authorised by Army Order 266 of 1919, amended in 1922. As the only silver medal in the First World War series, it comes closest to the style of earlier campaign medals, bearing the monarch's effigy and formal titles, and a symbolic design on the reverse. This is the medal that would have carried clasps, had they been approved.

The BWM is commonly seen accompanied by any of the other 1914–18 medals, but is the only one in the series that could be awarded by itself; such awards were earned by those who served overseas but did not enter a designated theatre of war – for example, doing routine garrison duty in India, the Far East, Sudan, South Africa, etc. Some were also awarded by themselves for service in the United Kingdom – most commonly to personnel of the Royal Navy who were mobilised for war service, to the Coast Guard or to the RNAS. The medal is also found paired with just the Victory Medal or the Mercantile Marine Medal or the Territorial Force War Medal.

The obverse adopts the existing 'coinage head' of King George V by Sir Bertram MacKennal with the abbreviated titles 'GEORGIVS V BRITT: OMN: REX ET IND: IMP:' but without the usual 'D.G' and 'FID. DEF'. The reverse was designed by W. McMillan, whose initials are visible on the reverse, lower right. It has the dates '1914' and '1918' above a scene in which a naked warrior on horseback tramples the emblems of the Central Powers, while the sun breaks through. The sea is just visible in the background. The mounted warrior is apparently meant to symbolise man's control over the forces of war, though it has been claimed to be simply an adapted image of St George.

The BWM is machine-impressed (not hand-engraved) around the rim in a variety of styles, mainly sans-serif block capitals of varying widths and heights, since the medals were named in different places; those to African personnel are often found in a variety of locally impressed, often uneven, types, whilst those to Indians were named in the Calcutta Mint. The details normally give the number, abbreviated rank, initials, surname and

Left: The British War Medal, obverse, with ribbon.

Right: The British War Medal, reverse.

abbreviated unit of the recipient. Those to Army officers give only the rank, initials and surname – not the unit. It was intended that the unit named on the medal would be that with which the recipient entered a theatre of war, thus qualifying for the award, though this does not seem to have been applied in a hard and fast way and some show the recipient's later unit. Medals to the Navy and Marines have 'RN' or other branch abbreviations ('RNR', 'RNVR', 'RMLI', 'RMA', 'MFA', etc.), not the names of ships, and those to aerial forces have 'RFC', 'RNAS' or 'RAF'.

The watered ribbon, 32mm wide, has a wide central band of orange, flanked with thin stripes of white, black and blue; it has no heraldic or symbolic significance and is carried from a straight, undecorated, non-swivelling suspension bar.

Since around 6,500,000 of these were issued – they were also awarded to all Imperial forces – this is the commonest British campaign medal.

## THE BRITISH WAR MEDAL IN BRONZE

Bronze versions of medals were awarded in earlier Imperial campaigns to African and Indian non-combatants – 'followers', servants, porters, etc. – who had gone on active service with military forces. In India the system had been applied since the mid-nineteenth century, and bronze versions of the appropriate medals were also awarded to Sudanese and other African non-combatants for service in some of the smaller African campaigns. The issue of a British War Medal in bronze to non-combatants simply followed this precedent but it was the last time that such an award was made; after 1918, all recipients of medals, combatant or not, received the same type.

The reverse of the British War Medal in bronze.

The bronze medal was identical in all respects to the silver version and was awarded largely to those who had served as porters and labourers behind the lines or in depots and ports in the various Indian Labour Corps (e.g. Peshawar Labour Corps), the Chinese, Maltese and South African Labour Corps, and in the Macedonian and Maltese Mule Corps. It was not awarded with a Star or the Victory Medal. They were usually named in the normal way, but some are found with only the recipient's number (not name) and abbreviated unit.

Although approximately 240,000 were issued, this is a scarce medal and is rarely seen with other awards.

**Above left:**
An example of
the early dull or
matt version of
the Victory Medal.

**Above middle:**
The gold-washed
British Victory
Medal, obverse.

**Above right:**
The British Victory
Medal, reverse.

## THE VICTORY MEDAL

The British authorities agreed at the Versailles Conference in 1919 to award a medal, standardised with those of other Allies, to all those who had 'entered a theatre of war'. It was authorised by Army Order 301 of 1919, with amendments into 1923.

The bronze medal was the standard 36mm in diameter. The first types, once wrongly regarded as special officers' versions, were of dull, matt bronze, but this type was discontinued by December 1920, to be replaced by the more familiar version coated with a thin gold wash. This coating was easily removed by polishing or wear, and the medal was regarded by many as a cheap and tawdry object, unworthy of the service and sacrifice it commemorated. Since around 5,725,000 were issued to British and Imperial forces, it is one of the commonest British medals.

The Victory Medal was designed by W. McMillan, whose initials are embossed on the obverse, lower right. He also designed the British War Medal and submitted a highly commended design for the Memorial Plaque (q.v.). As with most other Allied versions, it bore on the obverse a winged Victory, without wording. The reverse simply has 'THE GREAT WAR FOR CIVILISATION 1914–19' in a wreath, the dates being extended to 1919 to cover service during the British intervention in the Russian Civil War.

The ribbon, rather wider than usual at 37mm, was standardised with those of the other Allied versions as a series of stripes comprising a 'double rainbow'. It is carried by a small brass ring attached to a mount fitted directly to the medal.

The medal is machine-named (sometimes very faintly) in the same way as the British War Medal;

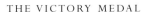

**Left and above left: 'As issued':** medals arrived in the post contained in a small, named card box, each medal in an envelope accompanied by a folded length of its ribbon.

awards to Indian soldiers are sometimes found unnamed, perhaps because of the scale of the task of naming them individually and getting them to their recipients in a reasonable time.

It should be noted that this medal was never awarded by itself: it is always found with at least the British War Medal, and any others the recipient might have earned.

## THE SOUTH AFRICAN VICTORY MEDAL

The Victory Medal awarded to personnel of the Union of South Africa was identical to that awarded to other British and Imperial forces except that it had a variant reverse. The standard wording appeared in English as 'THE GREAT WAR FOR CIVILISATION', with an added Dutch version below: 'DE GROTE OORLOG VOOR DE BESCHAVING 1914–19'. It is estimated that about 75,000 were awarded.

Variant versions were not produced for other Imperial territories: Canadian recipients might have had an added French text, or Indians might have had one in Hindi or Urdu.

Below: A group of miniature awards. '1915 Trio' with Second World War Defence Medal (coin for scale). These were worn on formal occasions in place of the heavier full-size versions.

Above left: The reverse of the South African Victory Medal.

Left: The '1914–15 trio', sarcastically nicknamed 'Pip, Squeak and Wilfred', after three newspaper cartoon characters, by those who thought them unworthy of the service they represented.

The 'lifeline of the Empire': a convoy of merchant ships and troop ships protected by warships.

## THE MERCANTILE MARINE MEDAL 1914–18

Unlike the other 1914–18 awards, the medal authorised for the Merchant Navy in July 1919 was administered by the Board of Trade. As in the Second World War, the Merchant Navy played a crucial role in 1914–18, with convoys maintaining shipments of food and armaments to the United Kingdom and carrying troops and supplies to all parts of the world in the face of an effective German submarine campaign. Associated with them in doing a vital job at sea were the fishing fleets, lightships and pilot service.

The bronze medal, the usual 36mm in diameter, was given to those who completed one or more voyages through a designated 'danger zone'. Although approximately 250,000 Mercantile Marine Medals were awarded, they are scarcer than most of the other general awards. The medal could not be conferred by itself and is usually seen paired with just the British War Medal, but it could be awarded with others (e.g. the 1914–15 Star and Victory Medal) if the recipient also qualified through additional service in another unit (commonly the Royal Navy). This means that some recipients wore four medals for 1914–18 service. If worn with a group, the Mercantile Marine Medal was worn between the British War Medal and the Victory Medal.

Below:
The Mercantile Marine Medal, obverse, with ribbon.

Below right:
The Mercantile Marine Medal, reverse.

The obverse bears the MacKennal effigy and titles as on the British War Medal. The reverse was designed by Harold Stabler, whose initials are to be seen on the reverse design, lower right, and features a crowded and dramatic view of a merchant ship ploughing through heavy seas. A submarine sinks in

A group containing the '1915 trio' with the Mercantile Marine Medal – the maximum that could be earned for 1914–18 campaign service.

the middle ground and a sailing vessel passes in the distance. It bears the wording 'FOR WAR SERVICE / MERCANTILE MARINE / 1914–18'.

The colourful ribbon – half red and half dark green, separated by a thin white stripe – represents the port (red) and starboard (green) lights of a merchant ship and its white masthead light. It is carried from a straight, undecorated, non-swivelling suspension bar.

The Mercantile Marine Medal (and the British War Medal awarded with it) is named in square, sans-serif block capitals with just the recipient's name, without rank, ship or other details. Unusually, the first name is generally stated in full (e.g. 'JOHN M. JONES'). Those to Australian personnel have only the recipient's initials and surname but also carry the word 'AUSTRALIA' and the recipient's service number after the name.

## THE TERRITORIAL FORCE WAR MEDAL (TFWM)

This bronze medal, the standard 36mm in diameter, was rather belatedly authorised by Army Order 143 of 26 April 1920 for members of the Territorial Force and TF Nursing Service, the forerunners of the Territorial Army. It had quite complex award criteria. It was conferred on *existing* members of the Territorial Force who had volunteered prior to 30 September 1914 to serve overseas and had then done so. In addition, recipients had either to have been members of the TF on 4 August 1914 or must have completed four years' service before that date and then rejoined not later than 30 September. In addition to all this, they must not have qualified for either the 1914 Star or the 1914–15 Star. Many Territorial units did of course qualify for one of the bronze stars. The TFWM is scarce to some units (e.g some Yeomanry regiments), since comparatively few of their members

Below left:
The Territorial Force War Medal, reverse.

Below:
The Territorial Force War Medal, obverse, with ribbon.

met its qualification terms. Only around 34,000 were awarded in total, making it the rarest of the general awards for 1914–18.

The obverse bears the standard royal effigy and titles as on the British War Medal, while the reverse has the simple wording 'FOR VOLUNTARY SERVICE OVERSEAS 1914–19', enclosed by a wreath of laurel. Above the wreath is the additional wording 'TERRITORIAL WAR MEDAL'. It should be noted that despite the dates '1914–1919' on the reverse, entitlement actually ended on 11 November 1918 – unlike the Victory Medal, whose similar dates were included to incorporate service in the post-war Allied intervention in the Russian Civil War.

The medal could not be awarded by itself but is seen at least with the British War Medal (the two granted for overseas service *not* in a theatre of war, e.g. garrison duty in India and elsewhere) or additionally with the Victory Medal if the recipient did enter a designated war zone. Members of the Territorial Force therefore received two or three medals for campaign service. The TFWM was named in machine-impressed block capitals, with number, abbreviated rank, initials, surname and abbreviated unit, and was worn after the British War Medal or after the Victory Medal, if the latter had been awarded.

The watered ribbon has stripes of yellow and dark green, the yellow recalling the Imperial Yeomanry long-service medal ribbon, and the green that of the old Volunteers' long-service medal. It is carried from a straight, undecorated, non-swivelling suspension bar.

Below:
The Territorial Force War Medal worn in pair with the British War Medal. The recipient of this pair served only in South Africa.

Below right:
The reverse of the TFWM and BWM pair, showing a typical privately purchased medal mounting bar.

# DESIGNATED THEATRES OF WAR

THE BRITISH WAR MEDAL and the Territorial Force War Medal could be awarded for overseas garrison duty (e.g. in India, Malta, Gibraltar, Singapore, South Africa, the West Indies, Hong Kong, the Sudan or Burma) without the recipient having to enter a 'theatre of war'. All the other awards required that the recipient had entered a designated war zone.

The 'approved' theatres were laid down in detail, with defined geographical and time limits; those below are the basic areas and dates, with the major theatres shown in bold. They demonstrate conclusively that for Britain this was a world war, and not restricted just to the familiar trench lines of the Western Front.

WESTERN EUROPE
**France and Belgium**: 5 August 1914 to 11 November 1918
North-east Italy: 17 April 1917 to 11 November 1918

BALKANS
**Greek Macedonia (Salonika)**, Serbia, Bulgaria and European
    Turkey: 4 October 1915 to 11 November 1918
**Gallipoli** and the Aegean Islands: 24 April 1915 to 9 January 1916

RUSSIA
Russia: 4 August 1914 to 1 July 1920 (into the Russian Civil War)

EGYPT
Egypt: Suez Canal defences and Western Desert: 4 August 1914 to
    18 March 1916
**Egyptian Expeditionary Force** (Palestine): 19 March 1916 to
    11 November 1918

AFRICA
**British, German and Portuguese East Africa**, Nyasaland and
    Uganda, 19 August 1914 to 25 November 1918

German South West Africa: 19 August 1914 to 9 July 1915
German West Africa – German Kamerun (Cameroon): 23 August 1914 to 18 February 1916
German West Africa – German Togoland: 6 August 1914 to 26 August 1914
West Africa – French/German West African frontier: 4 January 1917 to 15 May 1917

In action on the Western Front: 'L' Battery at Néry, 1914.

ASIA

Hedjaz (Arabia): 4 November 1914 to 11 November 1918

**Mesopotamia**: 5 November 1914 to 11 November 1918

Bushire (Persian coast): 27 June 1915 to 11 November 1918

South Persia and Persian Gulf ports: 5 November 1914 to 11 November 1918

Muscat (Persian Gulf): January 1915

Seistan (East Persian frontier): 1915

Shaik Saad (South-west Arabia): 10–11 November 1914

Perim (South Arabia): 14–15 June 1915

**Aden and hinterland**: 3 July 1915 to 11 November 1918

North West Frontier of India: Tochi Valley: 27 November 1914 to 27 March 1915

North West Frontier of India: Hafiz Khor area (Mohmand): 13–19

Landing on Gallipoli in 1915: troops coming ashore from the *River Clyde*.

April 1915, and/or 28 August to 10 December 1915, and/or
28 August 1915 to 10 November 1915, and/or 29 September
1916 to 19 July 1917
North West Frontier of India: Swat Valley area: 16–31 August 1915
North West Frontier of India: Landakai Ridge (Malakand):
20–31 August 1915, and/or 27 October 1915
North West Frontier of India: Mahsud operations (Waziristan):
1 March 1917 to 10 August 1917
North West Frontier of India: Marri operations (Baluchistan frontier):
17 February to 8 April 1918
North West Frontier of India: Khelat (Kalat) State: 4 June to 18 August
1916
North East Frontier of India: Chin and Kuki Hills: 30 December 1917
to 1 June 1918, and/or 31 October 1918 to 15 May 1919
North East Frontier of India: Kachin Hills: 30 December 1914 to
28 February 1915
Chinese coast: German Tsingtau: 22 September to 7 November 1914

AUSTRALASIA
German Pacific territories: New Britain: 10–21 September 1914
German Pacific territories: New Ireland: 15 September to 18 October
1914
German Pacific territories: Kaiser Wilhelm-Land: 24 September 1914
German Pacific territories: Admiralty Islands: 21 November 1914
German Pacific territories: Nauru: 6 November 1914
German Pacific territories: German Samoa: 29 August 1914

In the Far East,
1915.

# THE 1914–18 MEMORIAL PLAQUE

Tㅐᴇ ʙʀᴏɴᴢᴇ Memorial Plaque, granted to the designated next of kin of those from Britain and the Empire who died in service, is a familiar relic from the aftermath of the First World War. The idea that the government would issue a memorial to commemorate personnel who had died on war service was completely novel, and the fact that such a memorial, paid for by the state, was even considered is a testimony to the extent to which the 'Great War' had affected people and families on a greater scale than ever before and had drawn in the whole nation and Empire.

A government committee was set up in October 1916 to examine the production of a personalised memorial, the idea being publicised in *The Times* in November as a 'Memento for the Fallen. State Gift for Relatives'. Chaired by the Secretary of the War Office, it comprised thirteen members of the Houses of Lords and Commons representing government departments, including the Indian, Dominion and Colonial Offices. It was decided that a named bronze plaque best fitted the plan, and a public competition was announced in August 1917, with prizes for the winning designs. To help with design issues, the directors of major galleries were co-opted, including those of the Victoria and Albert Museum, the National Gallery and the British Museum's Department of Coins and Medals.

Detailed instructions were laid down as to size and materials: it was to be no more than 18 inches square (or 4.75 inches in diameter if circular) and was to incorporate a symbolic figure and suitable inscription. The latter was settled as 'He (or She) died for freedom and honour', as well as the name (only) of the deceased; a key requirement was that 'the design should be essentially simple and easily intelligible'.

Details of the competition were published in *The Times* in August 1917 and attracted great interest. In October it was decided that an Illuminated Scroll, designed 'in house' without public consultation, would also be presented with the plaque. The wording was carefully considered and that proposed by Dr M. R. James of King's College, Cambridge (now more famous for his ghost stories) was chosen.

The bronze Memorial Plaque, often found mounted in privately purchased unofficial decorative frames of many different types.

Over eight hundred plaque designs were submitted from artists at home, from the Empire and from many fronts of the war. The finalists' entries were submitted to the War Office and Admiralty (the King also being consulted), and the results were published in *The Times* in March 1918. The winning design was the work of the Liverpool sculptor Edward Carter Preston (winning the respectable sum of £250) and depicted a figure of Britannia in mourning, proffering a wreath, with two dolphins (representing sea power) and the 'British lion' in the foreground. Carter Preston (1885–1965) became a familiar name in medal design; he also designed the reverse of the General Service Medal 1918–62, the 1939–45 War Medal and the Korean War Medal.

Other prize-winning entries were supplied by the Chelsea sculptor Charles Wheeler and by W. McMillan (who designed the British War and Victory medals) and others. Nineteen other 'commended' artists were named in *The Times* and the leading entries were displayed in the Victoria and Albert Museum in the summer of 1918.

A description of the plaque was published in *The Times* in March 1918 and unsurprisingly, given its international significance, drew immediate comment, some of it critical. The lion ('which a hare might insult') and the proportions of the figure and animals were particularly criticised. However, attempts to alter the design (apart from changes resulting from practical problems with die production) did not succeed and the artist prevailed.

The heavy card box of issue for the Memorial Plaque.

An unofficial memorial card. Thousands of different types were produced to be sent by grieving families to friends and relatives.

Manufacture began in December 1918, after the associated scroll design and wording had been agreed. Production was carried out initially in a former laundry in Acton, London, but from December 1920 moved to Woolwich Arsenal, and may have been undertaken in other factories that had ceased war munitions production.

As originally designed, the 'H' in 'He died...' was a wide initial, but many are found with a narrower letter. Claims that the latter were awarded to naval casualties have no foundation since both varieties are found to the Army and the Navy; it is probably just a die variation. The designer's initials are shown by the lion's front paws, and a small number between or behind the lion's rear legs is a finisher's identification number, part of a system of batch control. Those with the number after the lion's legs (left as viewed) were produced at Acton; those with numbers between the lion's rear legs were produced at Woolwich Arsenal. Most of the latter carry on the reverse a combined 'WA' in a circle for Woolwich Arsenal, but many are unmarked.

From the beginning of 1919 as many as 1,360,000 plaques were issued, given not only in respect of the 900,000 or so British and Imperial service personnel who had died on active service, but also for anyone who had died on uniformed war service of any kind and through disease or accident. The official cut-off dates were 4 August 1914 to 30 April 1920, so that, as well as casualties of the world war, later deaths (e.g. from the effects of wounds) or casualties from the Russian Civil War, the Iraq Rebellion and operations on the North West Frontier of India were included. Some plaques are known to have been issued into the 1930s, probably simple 'late issues' or late claims. They could, of course, be presented by themselves, without associated campaign medals, for those who died on duty 'at home' or who had no overseas theatre of war service. Plaques worded 'She died...' (with production figures variously reported from six hundred to fifteen hundred) commemorated female casualties, mainly nurses, and often the victims of drowning on torpedoed or mined troop or hospital ships. These are very rare.

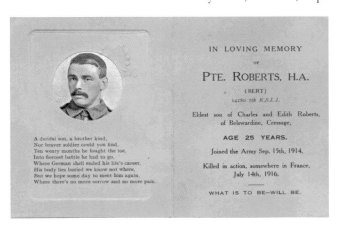

IN LOVING MEMORY

OF

PTE. ROBERTS, H.A.

(BERT)

14280 7th K.S.L.I.

Eldest son of Charles and Edith Roberts, of Belswardine, Cressage,

AGE 25 YEARS.

Joined the Army Sep. 15th, 1914.

Killed in action, somewhere in France, July 14th, 1916.

WHAT IS TO BE—WILL BE.

A dutiful son, a brother kind,
Nor braver soldier could you find,
Ten weary months he fought the foe,
Into fiercest battle he had to go,
Where German shell ended his life's career,
His body lies buried we know not where,
But we hope some day to meet him again,
Where there's no more sorrow and no more pain.

# OTHER BRITISH AWARDS

## THE SILVER WAR BADGE (SWB)

A COMMONLY SEEN ITEM is a lapel badge frequently called the 'wound badge' or 'discharge badge', but more accurately known as the Silver War Badge (SWB). Authorised on 12 September 1916, it was granted to anyone in British and Imperial forces who was discharged from the services on the grounds of wounds, injuries or sickness while on war duties at home or abroad. The convex badge, fretted in silver, is fitted with a pin to the plain reverse, which is stamped with an individual number – though it is not the recipient's service number. It is possible to trace the recipient via the reverse number using files held at the National Archives. Around a central royal cipher, 'GRI' surmounted by a crown, is the wording 'FOR KING AND EMPIRE / SERVICES RENDERED'. The award of one of these badges is indicated on the Medal Index Card (see page 36) with 'SWB' and a roll or page reference.

It is frequently claimed that these badges, intended to be worn on civilian dress, were conferred to stop men being harassed by women offering them white feathers for failing to do military service, but there is no foundation for this. It is much more to be seen as a simple and immediate recognition of 'services rendered' – as it says – before any other general awards were available.

## THE DISCHARGE SCROLL, 1916

In 1916 it was decided to award a large decorative 'Discharge Scroll' to those honourably discharged on the grounds of disability, wounds, illness, etc. There were three types, designed by Bernard Partridge, for Army, Navy and aerial forces. That most commonly seen is to Army personnel and features a British and a Colonial soldier presenting arms before an enthroned, martial figure of Britannia, surrounded by the names of the major dominions and colonies and other decorative devices. The other types (somewhat scarce) replace the figures of soldiers with airmen or naval personnel and appropriate background detail.

Below: The Silver War Badge, obverse.

Bottom: The Silver War Badge, numbered reverse.

The 'Honourable Discharge' scroll. (Army version.)

Below left: An example of a local Special Constabulary medal – in this case, for the Metropolitan Police.

Below right: The Special Constabulary Medal, with 'Great War' bar, obverse, with 'crowned and robed' effigy of the King.

Each certificate bears the recipient's number, rank, name and unit, entered in manuscript, followed by the printed wording 'Served with Honour and was disabled in the Great War. Honourably discharged on [date]'.

## THE SPECIAL CONSTABULARY MEDAL FOR THE GREAT WAR

During the war many local police forces enrolled part-time Special Constables to do extra police work (e.g. railway security, street patrols, etc.) or to free existing policemen to join the forces, and there are numerous examples of local police medals created to reward this work. In August 1919, in recognition of the national role of the 'Specials', the King authorised a Special Constabulary Medal. Claimants had to have worked voluntarily (without pay) for at least three years and have carried out at least 150 police duties. Although it was intended initially as a

war-service reward, it was retained as a long-service medal and is still awarded. Those who received the medal for 1914–18 service wore on the ribbon a small bronze bar with the words 'THE GREAT WAR 1914–18'. This is stitched on in the same fashion as the clasp for the 1914 Star.

The bronze medal has on the obverse the 'crowned and robed' effigy of George V – an attractive alternative – designed by Sir Bertram MacKennal, with the usual abbreviated titles. The reverse simply has the wording 'FOR FAITHFUL SERVICE IN THE SPECIAL CONSTABULARY' amid laurel sprays. The ribbon is red, flanked by equal stripes of white, black and white, and hangs from a straight, undecorated suspender. They are named around the rim in small impressed block capitals with the recipient's full name (e.g. 'HARRY JONES') and sometimes a rank but without specifying a force or district.

## THE INDIAN FRONTIERS

Although there was considerable fighting on the North West Frontier of India during the war – including a major campaign in Waziristan in 1917 – and occasionally on its North East Frontier, it was decided that these operations should be included in the general prosecution of the world war and would be rewarded with the standard war medals. British and Indian personnel who served in these operations could receive the 1914–15 Star, the British War Medal and the Victory Medal (or, depending on date, the last two only). Some may also have received the Territorial Force War Medal, if appropriate. Under any other circumstances, they would doubtless have been awarded the current (1908) India General Service Medal with an appropriate clasp, such as *North West Frontier 1915* or *Waziristan 1917*.

The rulers of many of India's princely states (e.g. Jaipur, Jodhpur, Patiala, Kashmir) sent their own forces to join the Indian Army on active service as Imperial Service Troops (IST), mainly in East Africa and Mesopotamia, and a number awarded their own 1914–18 war medals. Their personnel would also have received the British issues.

## THE KHEDIVE'S SUDAN MEDAL, 1910–18

Unlike the campaigns on the Indian Frontier, tribal operations in the Sudan during the war were not linked to the wider fighting but deemed to be separate local issues. British personnel who served *only* in the Sudan received the British War Medal alone (unless they also qualified for the Territorial Force War Medal): the Victory Medal did not apply since the Sudan was not deemed to be a theatre of war in world war terms.

An example of a 1914–18 medal from the Indian princely states: the service medal awarded by the state of Jaipur.

Above: The striking reverse of the Khedive's Sudan Medal (1910), with three clasps for 1914–18 service.

Above right: The obverse of the Khedive's Sudan Medal with clasp for *Darfur 1916*, showing the monogram of the ruler of Egypt, the Khedive Hussein Khamil; worn with the British War and Victory medals.

However, the existing Khedive's Sudan Medal (1910), conferred by the ruler of Egypt, could be awarded to those engaged in local expeditions. It was issued with the following clasps for operations which took place during the war:

*Miri*: for a rebellion in the Miri Hills, April 1915.

*Mongalla 1915–16*: tribal operations in the Imatong and Lafite Mountains.

*Darfur 1916*: large-scale operations against Sultan Ali Dinar.

*Fasher*: for actions around Fasher, part of the *Darfur 1916* operations.

*Lau Nuer*: for punitive operations against the Lar Nuer in 1917.

*Nyima 1917–18*: for punitive operations in the Nyima Hills against the Nuba.

*Atwot 1918*: for an expedition against the Atwot Dinka.

These are rare to British recipients since few British personnel were involved (mainly officers and senior NCOs with Sudanese units). The largest operations were in Darfur province in 1916, so that the most commonly seen clasps are *Darfur 1916*, sometimes with *Fasher*. These involved some British personnel (on a small scale) and are seen to the Royal Warwickshire Regiment, the Army Service Corps and the Royal Flying Corps. Most awards went to Sudanese and locally raised units, and most were unnamed; some were awarded without clasp, and there were bronze versions, now very rare, to non-combatants.

## THE AFRICA GENERAL SERVICE MEDAL (AGS) 1902–56

Instituted in 1902 to reward service in campaigns in east and west Africa, the AGS (unlike the Indian version) continued to be issued in the period 1914–18 for operations that were deemed to be local and not linked to the conduct of the world war.

The following clasps were issued for such expeditions between 1914 and 1918:

*Shimber Berris 1914–15*: for operations in Somaliland in 1914 and 1915.

*Nyasaland 1915*: for a rebellion in the Shire Highlands, January to February 1915.

*East Africa 1915*: for an expedition against the Turkhana tribe.

*Jubaland 1917–18*: for an expedition against the Aulihan tribe along the Juba River.

*East Africa 1918*: for operations against the northern Turkhana and other tribes.

*Nigeria 1918*: for the Egba Revolt in the area between Abeokuta and Lagos.

The Africa General Service Medal (1902) with one of its clasps for service during 1914–18.

These awards went mainly to local units (such as the King's African Rifles) and associated auxiliary forces, with few to British officers and NCOs. Some recipients may also, of course, have gained the 'general' war medals if they had served elsewhere; *Nyasaland 1915*, for example, is frequently seen with 1914–18 medals to soldiers who had also served in the East African campaign.

## THE RED CROSS WAR SERVICE MEDAL FOR 1914–18

In 1921 the British Red Cross Society awarded a medal to its personnel who had rendered one thousand hours of voluntary service during the war; most of this was for work in United Kingdom hospitals or nursing homes. The frequently seen small bronze-gilt medal, suspended from a plain white ribbon with an attached wearing brooch, is unnamed and was not intended to be worn with official campaign medals, or other than in Red Cross uniform.

The Red Cross medal for voluntary war service, obverse. The reverse has: 'INTER / ARMA / CARITAS' ('Amidst arms, charity') in a laurel wreath.

Several countries, including the United States and Serbia, also awarded separate medals for Red Cross War service.

## THE ALLIED SUBJECTS' MEDAL

After the war many foreign nationals were given the British War Medal in token of their assistance to British forces in the field (e.g. Belgian and French agents and interpreters); these medals were named and intended as something of a decoration rather than a simple 'campaign medal'. Foreign nationals might also be awarded British orders and decorations, though these were not usually named or gazetted. Nevertheless, in November 1920 it was announced that a distinctive medal would be awarded to foreign nationals – mainly French and Belgian – who had rendered exceptional humanitarian service, for example in helping British escaped prisoners. This was the Allied Subjects' Medal. A rare award, with only about seven hundred conferred, it was issued in silver

Above left:
The Allied
Subjects' Medal,
reverse, showing
the figure of
Humanity tending
a wounded soldier.
The obverse had
the usual head and
titles of the King.

Above right:
The obverse of
the silver Masonic
'jewel' for fund-
raising in the
'Masonic Millions'
campaign.

(134) or bronze (574) but regrettably was unnamed. About half were awarded to women. The ribbon — stripes of red, white, blue, yellow and black — incorporates the colours of the French and Belgian flags.

## THE MASONIC WAR MEDAL

A 'jewel' was awarded by and to Freemasons who contributed financially to the 'Masonic Millions' fund, established in 1919–20. Its aim was to pay for the building of a new Masonic headquarters as a memorial to those Masons who had died during the war. Given in gold or silver (according to donation), about 53,000 were awarded.

The reverse is flat and plain, except for hallmarks, and is usually engraved with the recipient's name, grade and lodge number. It hangs from a plain dark blue ribbon.

## MENTION IN DISPATCHES (MID) EMBLEMS

It had long been the custom to name in official campaign reports and dispatches those individuals who had rendered particularly gallant or distinguished service. For major campaigns, these lists were usually published in *The London Gazette*. Named individuals (usually only officers in earlier years) received no visible reward for the 'mention', though accelerated promotion in rank sometimes followed.

An Army Order of 12 January 1920 authorised a wearable emblem to those who had been 'mentioned', their names being published in *The London Gazette*. Because of its scale, the 1914–18 war produced over 141,000 official 'mentions'.

Numb. 29623.                                    5917

## SECOND SUPPLEMENT

*TO*

# The London Gazette

*Of TUESDAY, the 13th of JUNE, 1916.*

### Published by Authority.

*The Gazette is registered at the General Post Office for transmission by Inland Post as a newspaper. The postage rate to places within the United Kingdom, for each copy, is one halfpenny for the first 6 ozs., and an additional halfpenny for each subsequent 6 ozs. or part thereof. For places abroad the rate is a halfpenny for every 2 ounces, except in the case of Canada, to which the Canadian Magazine Postage rate applies.*

### THURSDAY, 15 JUNE, 1916.

*War Office,*
15th *June,* 1916.

The following despatch has been received by the Secretary of State for War from General Sir Douglas Haig, G.C.B., Commander-in-Chief of the British Forces in France:—

*General Headquarters,*
30th *April,* 1916.

SIR,—I have the honour to forward herewith the names of those under my command whom I wish to bring to notice for gallant and distinguished conduct in the field.

I have the honour to be,
Sir,
Your obedient Servant,
D. HAIG,
General, Commander-in-Chief
The British Forces in France.

ROYAL NAVY.

Dundas of Dundas, Vice-Admiral C.
MacGregor of MacGregor, Capt. Sir M., Bart.
Hamilton, Capt. D. M.
Marescaux, Cdr. (Acting Capt.) A. E. H.
Alton, Paymaster-in-Chief F. C., C.B.
De Montmorency, Capt. J. P.

Levitt, O.N.M.B.G. Chief Motor Boatman
H. W.
Axtell, O.N. 206939 (R.F.R. Po./B.6723)
A.B., E.
Wymer, O.N.J. 17246 A.B.; E. A.
Brett, O.N. 195033 (R.F.R., Chat./B. 7702),
A.B., W. J.

ROYAL MARINE ARTILLERY.

Lumsden, Maj. F. W., R.M.A.
Williams, Capt. M., R.M.A.
Brownrigg, Temp. Lt. A. H., R.M.
Lamb, Temp. 2nd Lt. F. R., R.M.A.
Handford, No. R.M.A./11901 Bombr. J.
Robins, No. R.M.A./10149 Bombr. W. T.
Orman, No. R.M.A./6809 Gunner A. E. E.
Guilford, No. R.M.A./14142 Gunner J. R.

ROYAL MARINE LIGHT INFANTRY.

Farrell, No. 24814 Acting Regtl. Serjt.-Maj.
J. (lent to Service Bn., Durham Light Infantry).

ROYAL NAVAL VOLUNTEER RESERVE.

Smith, Lt. C. A., D.S.O.
Stout, Lt. P. W.

STAFF.

Abbott, Capt. R. S., 38th Cent Ind. Horse
(Ind. Army).

A page from *The London Gazette* showing new 'mentions' for war service.

Above: The oakleaf spray emblem denoting a mention in dispatches, 1914–20, worn on the Victory Medal.

Right: An example of a certificate accompanying a 'mention', with the printed signature of Winston Churchill, then Secretary of State for War.

*The War of 1914-1918.*

*Shropshire Light Infantry*

*4404 S.M. S. G. Moore*

*was mentioned in a Despatch from*

*Field Marshal Sir John D. P. French, G.C.B. O.M. G.C.V.O. K.C.M.G.*

*dated 14th January 1915.*

*for gallant and distinguished services in the Field.*

*I have it in command from the King to record His Majesty's*

*high appreciation of the services rendered.*

*Winston Churchill*

*War Office*
*Whitehall S.W.*
*1st March 1919.*

*Secretary of State for War.*

The emblem took the form of a small oakleaf spray in bronze (awarded with a named and dated certificate for each mention), to be worn on the ribbon of the Victory Medal or, if this had not been conferred, on the appropriate service medal (e.g. British War Medal). Only one emblem was worn, no matter how many times the recipient was 'mentioned', and a half-size version was authorised for occasions when ribbons alone were worn. The award of an MID oakleaf spray is reflected on the Medal Index Cards (see page 36) by the word 'emblems'.

Awards were made retrospective to 4 August 1914, and in 1943 it was announced that 'mentions' after 14 August 1920 would be represented by a single bronze oakleaf. They are now awarded in silver.

## THE IMPERIAL SERVICE BADGE, 1912

A frequently seen award is the small white-metal badge worn from 1912 by members of the Territorial Force who volunteered for overseas service

The Imperial Service Badge.

– which was not their official function. Unusually, it was to be worn over the *right* breast pocket in uniform. Measuring only 4cm by 1cm, it simply has the words 'IMPERIAL SERVICE' below a crown; its reverse is plain, with a pin fitting, and it is not numbered or named.

## WAR SERVICE BADGES

Many industries and associations (notably armament and ordnance factories) issued armbands or badges to their staff to show that they were 'doing their duty' and undertaking war work. Most were plain or enamelled lapel badges, sometimes numbered on the reverse but usually unnamed, and they commonly bore the simple words 'WAR SERVICE' and sometimes an emblem or year. There is a large range of such badges, the most common being the oval or triangular brass types worn by women working in ordnance factories.

Above left: War Service Badge. Lapel badges like this dated example were worn by those doing war work but with no uniform or other identifying emblem to wear.

Above: A typical war worker's badge for the munitions industry. These badges were worn to show that the wearer was indeed contributing to the war effort.

## LOCAL TRIBUTE MEDALS

During and after the war, many local communities, from towns to hamlets, and some schools, businesses and other organisations, raised money to present what are called 'tribute medals' to local men and women who had served in the war. This followed a practice dating back at least to the Boer War of 1899–1902, for which similar awards are found. Most took the form of medallions or small medals of 'watch fob' type. Many were named to their recipients and some were finely designed and executed – but some were not. They vary enormously in size, materials and shape, and there is no catalogue of the many types. Few were awarded in quantity, and others (from small hamlets or small companies) were issued in ones and twos and are rare; previously unknown types still turn up. They could not, of course, be worn with official awards, and many ended up in drawers or on watch chains. Many communities presented similar 'Peace' or 'Victory' commemoratives in the form of medallions and medals.

Bottom left: Examples of named local 'tribute medals'. Left: a 'Peace and Victory' commemorative from Aston Ingham, near Ross-on-Wye, Herefordshire. Centre and right: tribute medals from Clive and Madeley, Shropshire.

Bottom right: An example of a French 'tribute medal', unnamed.

# RESEARCHING BRITISH CAMPAIGN MEDALS

MEDAL ENTITLEMENTS can be established through a number of original archives. The reader is advised to consult the website of The National Archives at Kew at www.nationalarchives.gov.uk, for research guides and a list of available rolls and records. Fees are charged to access records noted below as available via the National Archives website.

It should be borne in mind that tens of thousands of men and women served in uniform during the war but never went overseas or on active service (e.g. serving in Ireland, or on coastal or other United Kingdom defences); if a soldier did not 'enter a theatre of war' or serve overseas, he generally did not receive campaign medals.

## THE ARMY AND LAND SERVICES

There are two detailed original sources that establish the medal entitlement of an officer or soldier and other service categories (e.g. Army nurses): Medal Index Cards, and medal rolls.

### MEDAL INDEX CARDS

The Medal Index Cards (MIC), held at The National Archives in series WO.372, were compiled by the Army Medal Office after the First World War as an aid to the preparation and dispatch of campaign medals to their recipients. The whole process was efficiently carried out and few recipients seem to have been missed out – though late claims and late awards continued into the 1970s. Claims for replacement 1914–18 medals are no longer accepted.

The cards were intended to establish the fact of the recipient's entitlement to medals and record their dispatch, but they vary considerably in the information they offer. Generally, they give the recipient's service number, surname and initials, or sometimes full Christian names. They indicate the regiments or units in which he or she served and the ranks held by the recipient, and state which medals were awarded and dispatched.

Some cards are more informative than others, noting the theatre of war the person first entered (thus qualifying for medals) and the date – which is not the date of enlistment; they sometimes record that the recipient was killed, a prisoner of war, discharged or transferred to the Reserve (sometimes with date), and they usually record the award of the 1914 clasp, the Silver War Badge (SWB) or a Mention in Dispatches emblem, if appropriate. Some note the possession of a gallantry award or decoration.

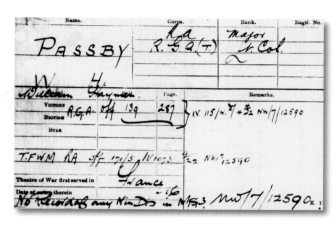

The index cards may be searched online via The National Archives website or for a fee from the website of Ancestry.co.uk. The latter is better – it reproduces both sides of the index card (and sometimes extra detail, such as the recipient's address, was added on the back) and they are clearer copies, reproduced in colour.

An example of a Medal Index Card, recording the award of the British War and Victory medals and the Territorial Force War Medal. Many are less detailed than this.

### MEDAL ROLLS

The original medal rolls were compiled regimentally or by the recipient's parent unit and sent to the War Office for processing. They are held in the National Archives under series WO.329 but are not available online at the time of writing. To access the person you are researching, you need to look first at the Medal Index Card (MIC); this gives the medal roll volume and page reference for each medal awarded and enables the researcher to order the appropriate roll on a visit to Kew. It should be said that the actual medal rolls are bland and uninformative – the MIC frequently offers more information – but they can be useful in establishing certain details, such as the exact battalion of a recipient, where the MIC often records only the regiment. For example, the MIC might record that a recipient served in the Cheshire Regiment, where the medal roll will state 6th Cheshire Regiment. This is useful if one wishes to follow the movements of the soldier during the war.

Apart from a few chance survivals amongst the British cards at Kew (e.g. some Indian soldiers' cards), there are no medal rolls in the United Kingdom for Imperial forces – Canadian, South African, New Zealand, Australian, Indian, etc.; these will be located in the national or military archives of those countries.

### NAVAL FORCES AND ROYAL MARINES

1914–19 medal rolls for the Royal Marines forces (Light Infantry, Artillery and other branches) have been made available at the website findmypast.co.uk

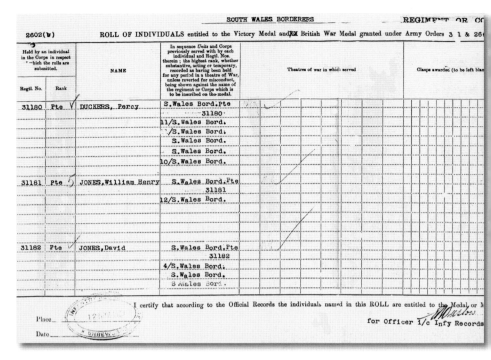

A page from a 1914–18 medal roll. They offer little detail.

There are no Medal Index Cards for the various naval forces. Their medals are listed only in the original medal rolls held in the National Archives under series ADM.171, which covers the Royal Navy, the Royal Naval Air Service (RNAS), the Royal Naval Volunteer Reserve (RNVR), the Royal Naval Reserve (RNR), and some other naval services (e.g. WRNS and canteen staff). These rolls are available online at ancestry.co.uk.

### AERIAL FORCES

Medal rolls for the Royal Naval Air Service, Royal Flying Corps and Royal Air Force are more scattered. Since many of their personnel were initially drawn from the Army or Royal Navy, most medal entitlements are included in the Medal Index Cards (WO.372) and medal rolls for the Army (WO.329) referred to above, which should be consulted, or the Royal Navy series ADM.171 for medal awards to the RNAS.

The Royal Air Force itself was not founded until 1 April 1918; there are no RAF medal rolls as such at Kew and only the personal service records will list the medal entitlement for those qualifying for medals after April 1918. Some entitlements may be found in the standard Medal Index Cards (see above), searchable online.

## MERCHANT NAVY

Medal cards prepared by the Board of Trade for Merchant Navy recipients of the Mercantile Marine Medal and British War Medal are held in the National Archives at Kew under series BT.351 and MT.9 and are available online via The National Archives website.

## PERSONAL SERVICE RECORDS

### ARMY

For regular and war commissioned officers of the land forces, papers are held in The National Archives under series WO.338, which also contains Royal Flying Corps officers' records. The records of Territorial Force officers are in WO.374. None of these series is currently available online.

For Army other ranks and related personnel, records are held at The National Archives in series WO.363 (personal records) and/or WO.364 (pension records). Because of official 'weeding', and damage during the Blitz, both series are fragmentary and many more are missing than survive. Usefully, the surviving records may now be searched online via Ancestry.co.uk for a fee.

Records of the Women's Army Auxiliary Corps (WAAC) are in WO.398 and available online at The National Archives website.

There are prisoner-of-war interviews and reports in WO.161, also available at The National Archives website.

### NAVAL FORCES

Royal Navy records survive in a much more complete state than do those for land forces. The service records for Royal Navy officers from c.1756 to 1925 are available in The National Archives under series ADM.196 or online via their website. Other ranks' personal papers from 1853 to c.1924, held in The National Archives under series ADM.188, are also available online via their website.

Above left: A Medal Index Card for the Mercantile Marine Medal. They are fairly bland.

Above: A page from an officer's service record for 1914–18 (in WO.338).

Records for the Royal Naval Reserve (in BT.164), for the Royal Naval Volunteer Reserve (in ADM.337), and for the Royal Naval Divisions (i.e. naval personnel serving ashore) in ADM.339 are all available online at The National Archives website.

Service records for the Royal Marines (both Royal Marine Light Infantry and Royal Marine Artillery) from *c*.1853 to 1935 are available at The National Archives in series ADM.159 or again online via their website.

The Women's Royal Naval Service (WRNS) records are in ADM.318 and 336 at The National Archives and are available online at their website.

Other ranks' service papers for the Royal Navy are useful in listing the ships served on, with dates. (ADM.188)

## AIR FORCES

At The National Archives, series AIR.76 (searchable online at their website) contains personal records for officers of the RFC and RAF who served prior to 1920, whilst AIR.79 has service records of other RAF personnel. Those to women (e.g. WRAF) are in AIR.80 and have been put online at The National Archives website.

RNAS officers' papers are in ADM.273 for service prior to March 1918, and then in the RAF series AIR.76.

Since many men of the RFC and RAF were originally drawn from the Army, it is worth checking in the Army series WO.363 and 364 for personal records. Similarly, for RNAS personnel serving prior to March 1918, the naval archive ADM.188 should also be consulted.

## OFFICERS' SERVICES

The promotions and appointments of officers (and periodically their 'war services' and awards) can be followed in officially produced lists such as *The Army List*, *The Indian Army List*, *The RAF List* and *The Navy List*. Sequences of these are available in The National Archives or may be found in larger town or city libraries or in military museums. Officers' promotions, appointments and awards for all services can be also found in *The London Gazette*, searchable online via www.gazettes-online.co.uk.

## HONOURS AND DECORATIONS

The easiest way to establish if a recipient was awarded an order, decoration or gallantry award (down to and including Mentions in Dispatches) is to consult *The London Gazette*, the official government newspaper, which published the fact of the award and sometimes (in a later *Gazette*) the citations for major honours. The *Gazettes* are searchable online at www.gazettes-online.co.uk.

A page from a 1914 *Army List*. These lists give officers' commission dates, promotion dates and appointments; some have 'war service' listings and details of honours and awards.

Most (but not all) awards of foreign decorations to British recipients were also 'gazetted' in the same way. *The London Gazette* also contains major dispatches – a useful contemporary source of information on campaigns and battles.

## CASUALTIES

Only service or pension papers (if they survive) will reveal whether, when and where someone was wounded, injured or gassed.

Those who were killed or died can be traced most easily via the 'Debt of Honour' database held by the Commonwealth War Graves Commission (CWGC) and searchable on their website, www.cwgc.org. This also gives cemetery or memorial locations and sometimes personal details, depending on what was originally offered to the CWGC by the next of kin. There are other official 'Rolls of Honour' and records of deaths (e.g. the War Office lists of 'Soldiers Died in the Great War'), which are available online, e.g. via Ancestry.co.uk, findmypast.co.uk and elsewhere.

An example of a regimental condolence card. Many regiments and units produced their own cards to send to bereaved next-of-kin and their families.

The Commanding Officer and Officers of
7th Battalion King's Shropshire Light Infantry
offer their deepest sympathy in the loss of
No. 205128 Pte Davies C.
Who gave his life for his King and Country.
21st August 1918.

AUCTO SPLENDORE RESURGO.

COMMANDING 7TH K·S·L·I·

# THE ALLIED
# VICTORY MEDAL

IN THE PAST, when Britain had fought in alliance with other countries (e.g. with Ottoman Turkey during the Crimean War of 1854–6, or in Egypt and the Sudan), British personnel had received awards from their allies, so that they wore both British and allied medals for the same campaign. Given the scale of the alliance system, if this had applied after the First World War it would have resulted in British personnel receiving numerous foreign medals and would have meant that the British authorities would have had to award possibly millions of British medals to our allies. This would have been an impossible financial and administrative burden.

It was therefore agreed at Versailles that the Allies would not give campaign medals to each other's forces. Instead, they would award a standardised Allied Victory Medal to their own personnel, each ally awarding

The Cuban Victory Medal: obverse and reverse.

Right: The Brazilian
Victory Medal,
obverse and
reverse.

Left: The United
States Victory
Medal, obverse,
showing army
clasps.

Right: The United
States Victory
Medal, reverse.

basically the same medal to its forces. The ribbon was standardised as a 'double rainbow' and the medal usually bore on the obverse an image of a winged Victory (*Nike*) or a similar allegory of victory. The Japanese, for example, had a mythical warrior on their version. The reverses were more varied, according to the wishes of the issuing country, and some featured, for example, the coats of arms and names of the victorious Allies.

Not all the Allies conformed to this system. Serbia, for example, had been incorporated into the new state of Yugoslavia, and Russia – a leading member of the allied coalition – did not award any official medals since her wartime ruler, the Tsar, and his government had been removed by revolution in 1917.

The rare Siamese Victory Medal: the distinctive obverse with the image of the God of War.

The following Allies issued a standardised Victory Medal between 1919 and 1923 (most of them also produced their own distinctive war-service medal or medals): Great Britain, the Union of South Africa, Belgium, Brazil, Czechoslovakia, Cuba, France, Greece, Italy, Japan, Portugal, Romania, Spain, Siam (Thailand) and the United States of America.

Apart from the British and South African issues, the medals are usually found unnamed, though some (American versions for example) were sometimes privately engraved.

The most interesting in the series is undoubtedly the American version, which became effectively their war medal for 1917–18 and was issued with a range of campaign, battle and service clasps. For the US Army, there were nineteen clasps – thirteen for campaigns (e.g. *Somme Offensive*, *Ypres-Lys* and *St Mihiel*), one general clasp, *Defensive Sector*, and five area clasps (*France*, *England*, *Russia*, *Italy*, *Siberia*) given to those who did not qualify for specific campaign clasps. In addition to some of these clasps, the US Navy and Marine Corps also had nineteen of their own, mainly 'branch of service clasps' such as *Escort*, *Mine Layer* and *Transport*, but also including area types such as *White Sea* and *West Indies*. Examples of the US Victory Medal are commonly seen with multiple clasps, though some are rare.

In some countries, such as France, the Victory Medals were made by a range of manufacturers, so that design variations may be found. Since some countries had only small contingents on active service (e.g. Cuba, Brazil, Thailand), some of these types were issued in small numbers and are rare. Because of their value on the collectors' market, the rarest types have been extensively faked, and great care should be exercised when purchasing the scarcer versions.

# ALLIES AND ENEMIES: SOME FOREIGN CAMPAIGN MEDALS

T HE MAIN PARTICIPANTS on the victorious side naturally issued their own
campaign medals for service during the 'Great War'. Unless otherwise
stated, the Allied Victory Medal was also awarded by these countries, and
some of the colonial powers, including Britain, France and Belgium,
continued to award medals for operations within their empires during the
period 1914–18 that were not related to the world war. What follows is a
selection of the main 1914–18 service medals of the combatant powers.

## THE ALLIED POWERS
### THE KINGDOM OF BELGIUM

The Belgians issued a range of general medals for 1914–18. The principal
award was the Commemorative Medal 1914–18, with, in common with
some other countries, a separate medal for those who had served voluntarily.

Left: Belgium:
War Medal:
obverse.

Right: Belgium:
War Medal:
reverse.

The Yser Medal (later Cross), instituted in 1918, was granted to those who had fought on the River Yser in the earliest days of the war, 17–31 October 1914; the original greenish-bronze medal was converted to a cross in 1934. In addition, there were medals for political prisoners, for those deported and for colonial service.

### THE REPUBLIC OF CZECHOSLOVAKIA

The newly established republic awarded the Medal of the Revolution in 1918 to members of the Czecho-Slovak legions who had served on the Western Front (largely the Alsace region), and in Siberia during the Russian Civil War. Slovakia, a Nazi puppet state in the 1940s, issued a Cross for the First World War in 1942. In gold and silver, each had three classes, but only the third class in silver was for campaign service, the other grades being for distinguished or gallant service.

Examples of Czech medals for 1914–18 service: the War Cross (a gallantry award), the Medal of the Revolution and the Czech Victory Medal.

### THE REPUBLIC OF FRANCE

France authorised the Commemorative Medal for the Great War (*Médaille Commémorative de la Grande Guerre*) in June 1920. Issued to all forces' personnel who had served at home or abroad between 2 August 1914 and 11 November 1918 and to civilian workers of many kinds, it was awarded to a far larger range of people than the equivalent British War Medal. Those who had volunteered for service wore a clasp *Engagé Volontaire*. As well as this and her own Victory Medal, France awarded between 1923 and as late as 1936 a range of medals for 1914–18: separate awards to *évadés* (escapees), to

Left: France: War Medal for 1914–18, obverse.

Right: France: War Medal for 1914–18, reverse.

47

those deported and interned, to 'victims of the invasion', and for service in the Dardanelles and Levant. During the war, France continued to award her existing colonial service medals for operations not related to the world war.

### THE KINGDOM OF GREECE

Greece conferred a silver War Cross. Established by the nationalist leader E. Venizelos in 1917, it was originally conferred only for gallantry but was later extended to become a general war-service award.

### THE KINGDOM OF ITALY

The Italian authorities issued both a general campaign medal for 1914–18 service and a medal to those whose service had been voluntary.

The Italian War Medal, issued in July 1920, showing King Victor Emmanuel III in Army uniform. These medals were said to have been produced from captured enemy guns.

### THE EMPIRE OF JAPAN

In addition to the Allied Victory Medal, Japan issued its own medal for the war with Germany, largely fought against Germany's Pacific colonies.

### THE KINGDOM OF PORTUGAL

Portugal, which had a relatively small contingent serving on the Western Front and forces engaged in East Africa, awarded two campaign medals, one for general overseas service 1914–18, and one for non-combatant service.

The Portuguese Victory Medal, obverse and reverse.

Far left: Serbia: retrospective medal, obverse, with effigy of King Peter I and ribbon in the old national colours.

Left: Serbia: retrospective medal, reverse, with the arms of Serbia.

## THE RUSSIAN EMPIRE

The empire of the Romanov dynasty vanished in the revolutions of 1917, and no general war medal was issued. However, in 1929 Russian monarchists in exile produced the Order of St Nicholas the Miracle Worker, which, despite its title, was actually a war-service medal for 1914–18. It could be purchased by veterans, the money going to aid the monarchist cause. Examples are rare.

An example of a National Guard medal for home service, 1917–18. This one was for the Pennsylvania National Guard. There are many different types.

## THE KINGDOM OF SERBIA

Serbia was incorporated into the new Kingdom of Yugoslavia after the Treaty of St Germain. She did nevertheless issue in September 1920 a bronze Commemorative Medal for the War of Liberation and Unity for veterans of 1915–18. It is sometimes referred to as a 'War Cross' because the circular medal is cut into in such a way that it resembles a cross.

## THE KINGDOM OF SPAIN

Apart from colonial medals (e.g. for Morocco) that were not related to the Great War, Spain awarded only the Allied Victory Medal to the relatively small numbers of its forces engaged (largely on the Western Front) during the war.

## THE UNITED STATES OF AMERICA

The USA awarded only the Allied Victory Medal as a general campaign medal for the First World War, though there were separate awards for service in Mexico, on the Mexican border and

Right: Austria: the Karl Troop Cross, obverse, with ribbon folded in the manner typical of Austro-Hungarian, Balkan and Russian awards.

Far right: Austria: retrospective War Commemorative Medal, obverse – 'For Austria'.

in Haiti and San Domingo in operations not related to the 1914–18 war. However, many medals for 1917–18 service were awarded by various states in their own name (e.g. to their National Guard units). These are regarded as local rather than national awards.

## THE ENEMY POWERS

The defeated powers, Germany, Austria-Hungary, Bulgaria and Turkey, were, unsurprisingly, not so quick to issue war medals, or in no condition to do so, but some eventually did in the inter-war years, when nostalgia and national pride began to reassert themselves. It was just as appropriate for them to reward the service of their forces as it was for the victors.

Right: Hungary: retrospective 1914–18 War Commemorative Medal, obverse.

Far right: Hungary: retrospective 1914–18 War Medal, reverse – 'For God and Country'.

## THE AUSTRO-HUNGARIAN EMPIRE

The Austro-Hungarian Empire was fragmented by the Treaty of St Germain in 1918 and Austria and Hungary issued few simple campaign medals for 1914–18 service, though their established gallantry awards were conferred during the war itself. The main Austrian campaign awards were the Karl Troop Cross (*Karl Truppenkreuz*), instituted by the new Emperor Charles (Karl) in December 1916 to reward one year's war service, and the War Commemorative Medal, inaugurated in December 1932 for issue to all ranks and services for 1914–18. Hungary, under its right-wing Regent, Admiral Horthy, instituted the War Commemorative Medal with Helmet and Swords in May 1929 for its veteran combatants, with a version without swords for non-combatant or home service.

Above left:
Bulgaria, War
Medal, reverse.

Above: Bulgaria:
War Medal, on
combatants'
ribbon, obverse.

## THE KINGDOM OF BULGARIA

Under King Boris III, Germany's ally Bulgaria awarded a retrospective medal in December 1933. The War Medal 1915–18 was given to all those who had served during the war and carried two types of ribbon, for combatant or non-combatant service. The medal was made available to Austrian and German veterans as former allies.

## THE OTTOMAN EMPIRE

The Ottoman Empire was broken up by the Treaty of Lausanne in 1923, its remnant becoming the Republic of Turkey, which did not confer a war medal.

During the war, the Sultan had awarded what was once called the Gallipoli Star or Iron Crescent. It is now known more generally as the Turkish War Medal. Several varieties of this pin-back breast badge exist. The standard issue was a poorly made flat metal star, simply painted in red, bearing the date 1915. Others are much better made (some in Austria or Germany, and some even in Birmingham) in white metal and red enamel. It is assumed that the latter were privately purchased by those – perhaps mainly officers – who did not think much of the original issue. Three clasps are associated with the award, possibly unofficially – *Chanaq Kila* (Gallipoli operations), *Qafqas* (Caucasus) and *Sinaq* (Sinai / Suez). It has been suggested that this star is a gallantry award rather than a simple campaign medal.

GERMANY

The Weimar Republic – the successor to the German Empire dismembered by the Treaty of Versailles in 1919 – awarded a retrospective Cross of Honour for the Great War. Instituted in July 1934 at the beginning of Nazi rule, but under the auspices of the Weimar president, Paul Hindenburg, one of Germany's greatest wartime leaders, it had three versions. The standard type was a flat cross of bronzed iron hung from a ribbon of red, white and black stripes – the commonly used Prussian colours. A blackened type was awarded

**Im Namen des Führers und Reichskanzlers**

Dem

     Maurer Hermann    A l b r e c h t,

                             B e r l i n

ist auf Grund der Verordnung vom 13. Juli 1934 zur Erinnerung an
den Weltkrieg 1914/1918 das von dem Reichspräsidenten Generalfeld=
marschall von Hindenburg gestiftete

**Ehrenkreuz für Frontkämpfer**

verliehen worden.

                       Berlin , den   17. Mai     1935.
                          Der Polizeipräsident.
                 Polizeiamt Pankow-Weissensee-
                    Prenzlauer Berg
                      I.V.

Nr. A. 649 /35.

Weimar Germany: award certificate for the Cross of Honour for combatants, dated 1935.

to the next of kin of those who had been killed or died during the war, and there was a version for non-combatants, without crossed swords.

The award was extended in 1938 to Austrian veterans, and in 1939 to those from Memel. Since up to eight million of the various types were awarded, it must be the commonest single medal for service in the Great War. The medals are not very impressive, but they did at least give some recognition to the veterans of Germany's armed forces and her allies.

Many of the old German states constituting the former German Empire – Bavaria, Saxony, Württemberg, etc. – issued medals during the war (often 'War Crosses'), but these were mainly for gallant or distinguished service rather than general campaign medals.

Bottom left: Weimar Germany: Iron Cross, Second Class with Cross of Honour. The Iron Cross was a Prussian (later German) gallantry medal, awarded in large numbers during the First World War.

Bottom right: A miniature of the Cross of Honour, worn (as is common with German awards) as a lapel badge, with additional ribbon of the Iron Cross.

# FURTHER INFORMATION

Those wishing to see large collections of medals of all types from the First World War should visit the main military collections in Britain, such as the Imperial War Museum in Lambeth, London, the RAF Museum in Hendon, the Royal Marines Museum in Southsea, or the Royal Navy Museum in Portsmouth. Other large unit museums include the Royal Engineers Museum at Gillingham and 'Firepower', the Royal Artillery Museum, at Woolwich. There are also more than 140 local regimental and military museums, many of which display collections of medals. Consult the detailed guide *Military Museums in the UK* by the Army Museums' Ogilby Trust (Third Millennium Publications, London, 2007). The Trust's website also provides details of military museums (see www.armymuseums.org.uk).

Useful research guides on military, family and medal records may be viewed or downloaded from The National Archives' website: www.nationalarchives.gov.uk.

OTHER USEFUL BOOKS:

Birch, D., Hayward, J., and Bishop, R. *British Battles and Medals.* Spink, 2006. This is the essential reference work on all British campaign medals from 1588 to date.

Dymond, S. *Researching British Military Medals: A Practical Guide.* The Crowood Press, 1999.

*Honours and Awards of the Army, Navy and Air Force, 1914–20.* Hayward, reprint 1979.

*Honours and Awards of the Indian Army, 1914–21.* Hayward, reprint 1979.

James, E. A. *British Regiments 1914–18.* Naval & Military Press, 1993. Wartime locations.

*Medal Yearbook.* Token, published annually.

Purves, A. A. *Collecting Medals and Decorations.* Seaby, 1978. Still useful on many levels.

Purves, A. A. *The Medals, Decorations and Orders of the Great War, 1914–18.* Hayward, 1975.

Rodger, N. A. M. *Naval Records for Genealogists.* HMSO, 1988.

Spencer, William. *Air Force Records for Family Historians.* Public Records Office, Kew, 2000.

Spencer, William. *Army Service Records of the First World War.* Public Records Office, Kew, 2001.

Spencer, William. *Medals: The Researcher's Guide.* National Archives, 2007. An essential guide to The National Archives' records.

Tapprell-Dorling, Captain H. *Ribbons and Medals*. George Philip, 1963;
    reprinted 1983. One of the first general works and still useful on
    non-British awards.
Williamson, H. *The Collector and Researcher's Guide to the Great War. Volume I*.
    Privately published, 2003. Highly recommended as a thorough guide.

Apart from archival websites like The National Archives, ancestry.co.uk
and findmypast.co.uk, useful sites are:

The Western Front Association: www.westernfront.co.uk
The Great War Society: www.thegreatwarsociety.com
World War One Trenches on the Net: www.worldwar1.com
The Long, Long Trail: www.1914–18.net/grandad

There are many others that a general battle or regimental search will reveal.

Medals, including
those for the
First World War,
on display at
Shrewsbury Castle
Museum.

# INDEX